Coventry

IN OLD PHOTOGRAPHS

Coventry

IN OLD PHOTOGRAPHS

DAVID McGRORY

A Budding Book

First published in 1994 by Alan Sutton
Publishing Limited

This edition published in 1998 by Budding Books,
an imprint of Sutton Publishing Limited
Phoenix Mill · Thrupp · Stroud · Gloucestershire
GL5 2BU

A catalogue record for this book is available from
the British Library

ISBN 1-84015-040-8

Typesetting and origination by
Sutton Publishing Limited.
Printed in Great Britain by
WBC Limited, Bridgend, Mid-Glamorgan.

For Dad —
a true Coventry kid born within the old city wall.

Contents

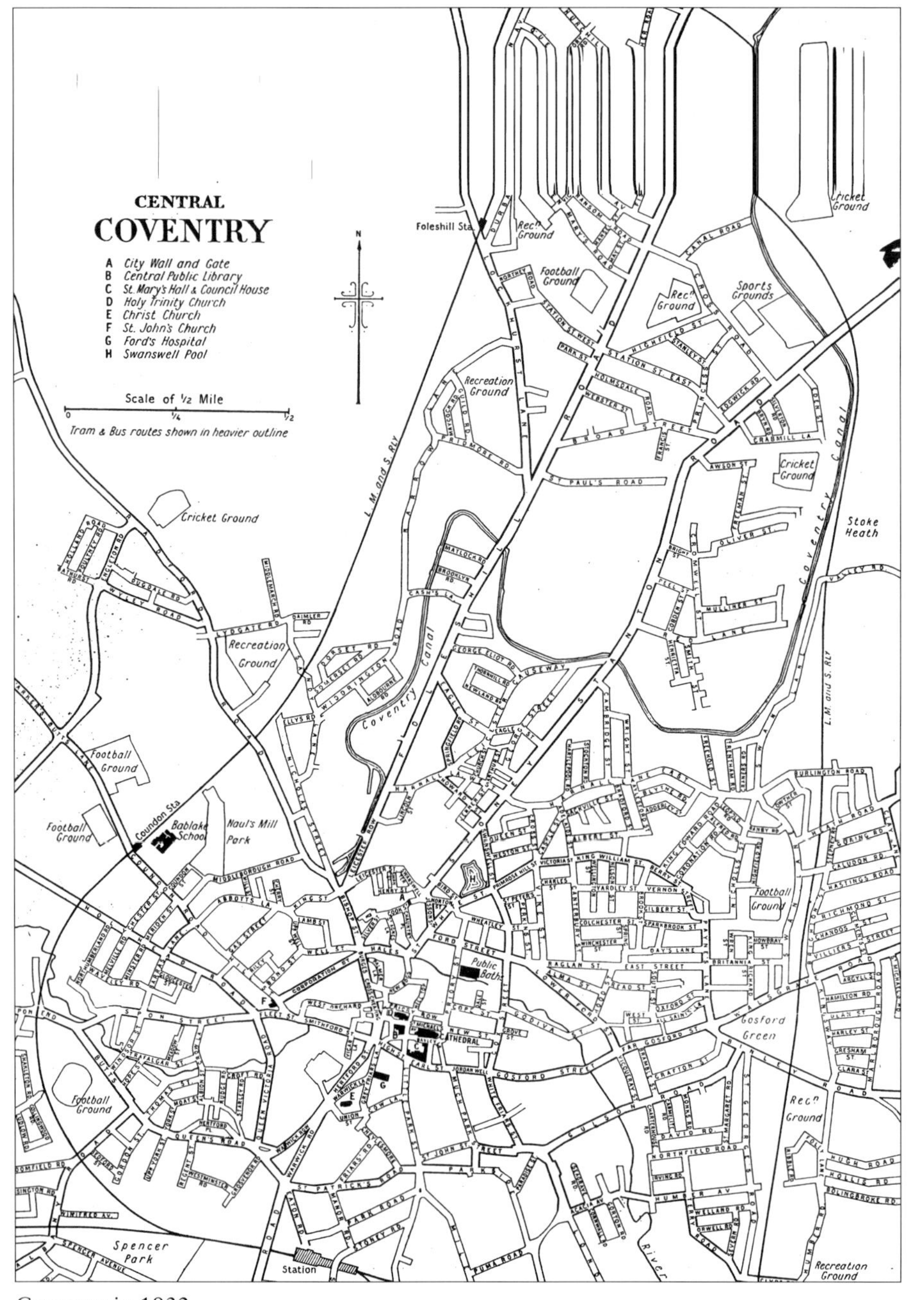

Coventry in 1932.

Introduction

In 1927 the notable and much-loved travel writer H.V. Morton described Coventry as an industrial centre 'spread like thick butter over a slice of medievalism'. Several of its buildings, including Ford's Hospital, St Mary's Hall and Bablake, were described by this worldly wise writer as the 'finest buildings of the kind in the world'.

What Morton saw was pre-Second World War Coventry before the destruction, a Coventry full of tiny streets, consisting of a jumble of buildings, ancient and modern, a medieval city hidden beneath brick and plaster façades. Archaeological discoveries were still being made in buildings such as the City Arms which stood on the site of the National Westminster Bank in Broadgate. Here, below an apparent nineteenth-century Georgian façade, lay a building begun in the fourteenth century, as its cellars testified. Inside there were fine fire-places and banisters, and other woodwork dating back to the sixteenth century. The centre of the city was full of large and small factories, many from the two previous centuries, which sat amid the huddle of ancient buildings.

Coventry was truly a mix of medieval and modern, but this began to come to an end with the mass destruction of buildings in Corporation Street during 1931 and the demolition of Great Butcher Row and Cross Cheaping in 1936. Smithford Street was to follow, but the bombs beat the planners. The wartime raids on Coventry cleared the way for the rebuilding of the city, and much that survived the bombs was unceremoniously laid waste in the name of progress and to aid the passage of the motor car.

Luckily the city's most notable ancient buildings survived, except for St Michael's Cathedral, Palace Yard and Spon chapel (which was reduced to a ruin). The destruction of old buildings still continued throughout the fifties and sixties, when rows of sixteenth-century buildings were not considered worth saving despite the great losses of the past. Notwithstanding fine gestures such as the preservation of Spon Street, little of what was later saved was rebuilt and one still feels that those in charge lack care for the old city, as buildings such as the old grammar school and a Georgian town house in Little Park Street are left to rot on their foundations.

The Coventry that Morton saw can still be found by simply walking from Broadgate into the Cathedral area. Here one can feel the difference, a strange feeling, almost like entering a different city. Likewise, when one enters Ford's

Hospital, described by Morton as 'the most beautiful and most loveable half-timbered building in England', one can feel, as he felt, that time itself has stood still.

The difference between Coventry now and in Morton's time (apart from the obvious) is that the city he saw still had its ancient roots close to the surface; now most of those roots have been tarmacked and concreted over and live only in the minds of those who know they're there. In his book *In Search of England* (Methuen, 1927) Morton described Coventry as a 'lucky city' for it had not suffered great destructive fires in the past as had London. Little did he know what the future had in store.

In this second selection of photographs of old Coventry I have changed the style from the first and followed the decades starting from the middle of the Victorian period. In this selection one can see the natural progression of time, especially in the numerous detailed views of Broadgate. The many scenes of devastation during the raids in the Second World War come as quite a shock after seeing so many scenes of a bustling city centre. Strangely, the foundation of this destruction was laid in 1870 with the birth of the cycle industry that led to the growth of Coventry as one of the country's most important manufacturing centres and therefore as a target in time of war.

In this book I have avoided as best I can repeating any information that was supplied in the first book, unless absolutely necessary for a full understanding of the particular picture or period. Many of the photographs have never before been published and constitute over two hundred excellent views of the city which in many ways no longer exists. Here, within the following pages, one may go on a journey into the past. I hope you enjoy it.

SECTION ONE

Victorian Coventry 1860–1900

A statuette of Lady Godiva created by William Behnes (1794–1864). This fine figurine may have been the one exhibited at the Great Exhibition of 1851. Inscribed with a line from Tennyson's 'Godiva' poem it now graces the Council House.

Lancers posing in Coventry Barracks in the 1860s between cannon captured during the Crimean War. The Russian guns arrived in the city in July 1858 and were described as being 'siege or fortress guns'. Both were cast in 1799, weighed around 40 cwt and measured 8 ft 2 in long. Both guns had seen service, been spiked and drilled afresh. They were later placed on Greyfriars Green (scrapped in 1943) and Swanswell.

Broadgate on a summer afternoon, *c.* 1875. Hackney carriages wait in the semi-deserted centre. Alexander, importer of wines and spirits, marks the beginning of Cross Cheaping and shows its side wall and windows, which would later be plastered over and bear the name Royal Vaults. This view remained unchanged until 1936.

ESTABLISHED 1748.

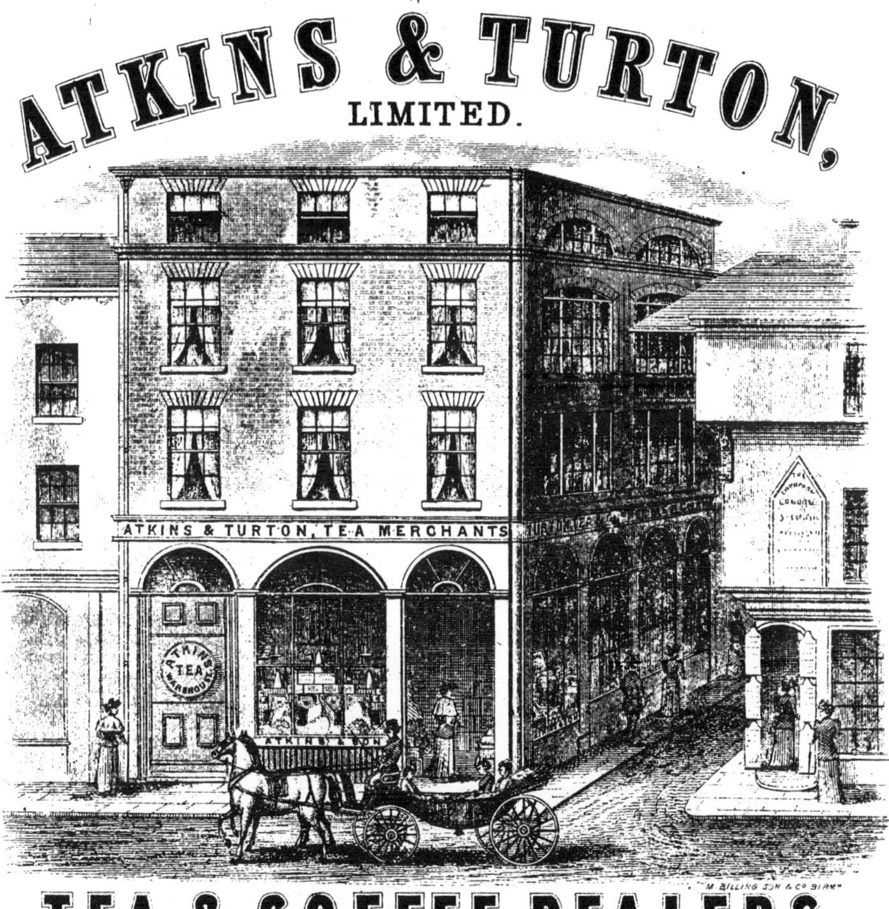

TEA & COFFEE DEALERS,

& FAMILY GROCERS,

HIGH STREET,

COVENTRY.

No. 2 High Street (1880), the premises of Atkins and Turton, tea and coffee merchants, on the corner of High Street and Pepper Lane, established in 1748 in what probably began life as a Georgian town house. The shop, which closed in the 1930s, left one indelible memory in the minds of many old Coventrians: the rich smell of roasting coffee beans. The shop front was changed, probably in the 1920s, and in March 1938 Martins Bank took over the premises and restored the frontage to its original condition. Later the building became a branch of the Coventry Building Society and was demolished in 1989.

An 1880 engraving copied from a photograph showing the premises of Fred W. Poole, tea, colonial and provision merchant, Nos 19 and 20 Fleet Street. Poole's business began in 1825 and in his shop and large warehouse to the rear he stocked produce from all over the world. This included tea and coffee; spices from the East; French and Italian pickles and preserves; ham and bacon from Wiltshire and America cured in the cellar; cheeses of England and France, including Poole's 'celebrated grand old Warwickshire Cheese'; Danish butter, eggs and fish; salmon from North America and herrings from Scotland; New Zealand mutton and lamb; tomatoes, asparagus and fruit from America; roast beef from New York; and much, much more. Mr Poole also acted as an agent for Messrs Gilbey who supplied him with assorted wines, spirits, champagne, etc.

A photo-engraving of The Stores (Nos 44 and 45 Cross Cheaping), the premises of Mr Herbert Lance, 1880. Established in 1860, The Stores had extensive stock which filled 'every nook and corner'. The shop was sectioned in two halves, No. 44 holding cloth, silk, wool, hosiery, haberdashery and drapery, and No. 45 trading as a gent's outfitter.

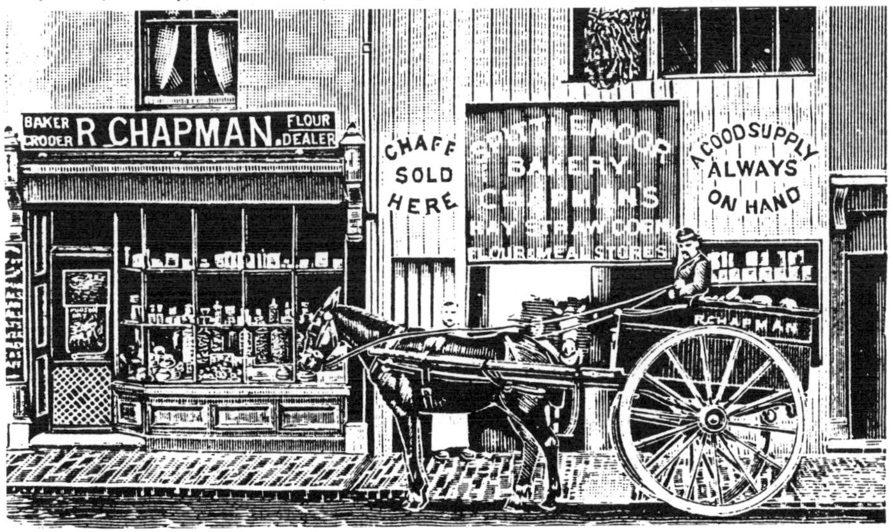

Photo-engraving of Randal Chapman's, baker and corn dealer, Hood Street, 1880. Apart from baking bread, for which Chapman 'was noted throughout the city', the dealership also had a warehouse attached in which was stored 'all kinds of corn, wheat, barley, oats, maize, Midlothian oatmeal, hay and straw, etc.'.

An 'Ordinary', probably built by the Coventry Machinist Co. in King Street, *c.* 1880. The company was highly successful and produced thousands of cycles based on designs by James Starley and William Hillman. Experts on the 'Ordinary' or 'Penny farthing' found these machines fast and highly manoeuvrable despite their looks. They could turn on a sixpence, or stand still as demonstrated in this photograph taken on the Radford Road.

Local children posing before Whitefriars Gate, 1875. This outer-gate to Whitefriars monastery was built in 1352 and originally had two figures in the recesses above the archway. The Gate was occupied as a dwelling from the seventeenth century until 1936. In this Victorian view the boards in the archway advertise J. Parsons, shoeing and jobbing smith. The Gate was restored in 1962 and again in 1971 and two years later became a toy museum.

Bablake School (founded 1560) and Bond's Hospital (founded around 1509) in Hill Street, *c.* 1880. In the middle right lies Bond Street which followed the line of the old city wall. The street marks the point in Hill Street where one of the minor city gates stood, which was known as Bablake or Hill Street Gate. The name Bablake is derived from the Celtic word *Babbu-lacu*, the Bab-lake, a huge lake which once covered the whole of the valley which lies on the north side of the city. This lake is thought to have been 30 to 40 ft deep in parts and ancient remains such as coracle paddles and a boat carved from a log suggest the lake was not unkown to ancient man. Until the River Sherbourne was culverted part of the old lake area was liable to flooding, reminding people of the site's past. The lamp on the right belongs to The Newdegate Arms which is recorded in the Coventry Directory in 1884 but not in 1850. The larger cobbles by the inn mark the entrance to Court 3 where my own father and grandfather were born.

St John's church, Fleet Street. This photograph, although originally taken around 1890, is from a postcard posted 26 June 1921. The postcard reflects the once regular migration of workers into Coventry and is sent care of Mrs Lovegroves, No. 85 Lower Ford Street, to a Miss Graham of Manchester. The card is sent by Harry, probably to his intended, and simply says, 'Just to let you know I landed alright about twelve o'clock. It is a fine works but have not had time to look round it yet.' As the card shows the top of Spon Street, no doubt Harry's new works was the Rudge-Whitworth factory at the bottom of the street.

Greyfriars Green probably from the roof of now-gone Stoneleigh Terrace, *c.* 1885. The Green began life as Lammas land on which Coventry's freemen held rights to graze cattle. The first house was erected in Warwick Row (left) in 1764 on the site of an old brick kiln. Where the statue of Sir Thomas White stands (erected 1882) was once the ducking pool used in past centuries for punishing unruly scolds on the city's own

ducking stool. By this pool once stood an elm tree under which two men were killed in the last century, struck dead by lightning. The pasture rights to the Green were relinquished in 1875 and the area tidied up and landscaped. The Quadrant on the right was completed on the site of an old orchard in 1863. Beyond this view lay nothing but countryside.

Little Butcher Row, *c.* 1890. The 'Frystar Cocoa' sign in the shop window of William Bird, grocer, could still be seen there forty-five years later. The buildings on the right date from the fifteenth century and those on the left, if not refaced, date from the eighteenth century.

The courtyard of Ford's Hospital, Greyfriars Lane, 1890. Some of the residents sit in the quiet courtyard with the hospital's pet parrot.

Looking down the nave of St Michael's, 1890. The nave contains pews which would later be replaced by chairs. The church was still a parish church, in fact the largest in England, being 24,015 sq ft, some 750 sq ft larger than its nearest rival St Nicholas' in Great Yarmouth.

The original Craven Arms, High Street, 1890. Described as Coventry's oldest hotel, it was noted for its 'comfort' and not for show. Dan Claridge completed twenty-one years as landlord of the inn on 6 March 1891. On this date the inn was described as having 'several principal suites of apartments, various private sitting rooms, some thirty bedrooms (all lofty and spacious), comfortable smoking room, coffee and commercial room [second floor balcony] and well-appointed billiard rooms.' The inn also had a large assembly room which was often used for auctions, meetings, concerts and dinner parties. It was also a political headquarters and meeting place for the Trinity and Stoneleigh Masonic lodges. Dan Claridge ran a hire service for 'coaches, barouches, landaus, cabs, cars, and wedding carriages'. Also for hire was his old stagecoach called *Olden Times* which Dan himself drove. This coach was the last ever to be driven (by Dan) from Coventry to London. The inn began life as The Bear Inn and was renamed in honour of Lord Craven in 1811. Thereafter it bore the arms of the Craven family above its door.

These buildings in Hertford Street (*c.* 1900) began life in the nineteenth century as Messrs Wyley & Co., chemical manufacturers. From their windows drifted the smell of ginger and rhubarb, two of the principal ingredients for the company's famous 'Gregory's Powder'. The buildings were then acquired and converted by Johnson and Mason, wine and spirit merchants and dealers in fine ales. Trading began in September 1885 with the warehouse to the right, seen here loading wagons with barrels, and to the left the offices and shop, supplying the passing public's needs. The building on the far right is the post office which still stands minus its fourth floor which was demolished to make way for the National Provincial Bank and Bank Chambers in 1929.

The packing department of Johnson and Mason, 1895. Here, the firm's whiskies, brandies, wines, ales, stouts, bitters, ciders, lagers and cigars were packed and loaded ready for delivery.

Johnson and Mason's wine cellar, 1895. This was just part of the massive 150 ft long vault which ran the whole length of the building at a depth of around 50 ft. Here were kept the finest wines from around the world and the finest ales and stouts. During the Second World War the city's war operations were controlled from here.

Men and horses posing in Johnson and Mason's stables in Greyfriars Lane, 1895. These stables were erected a year earlier at a cost of £2,000. Here were housed twelve horses and drays, and (left) a harness room and hay and corn store. Beneath this stable block Johnson and Mason extended their cellars, adding storage space for two hundred more barrels.

The London and Midland Bank on the corner of High Street and Little Park Street on its opening, June 1896. The bank's original joint managers, Mr Mellor and Mr Read, were still in charge of the bank in 1936.

The original, Victorian-Gothic Coventry and Warwickshire Hospital (built 1864–5) from the island in the centre of Swanswell Pool, *c.* 1895. In the early nineteenth century the pool was still a place of leisure. It was much larger than it is today, and every hour steam-powered paddle boats took customers around it.

Girls at work in the mending room in the roof space of Leigh Mills, Hill Street, 1890. The mill was set up mainly by Lord Leigh after the collapse of the ribbon weaving industry in 1860. The distress caused by the collapse led to four thousand Coventrians emigrating abroad.

The Quinton Works building department, 1896. These works, unlike many of Coventry's cycle factories, employed few workers: only two hundred (Rudge employed two thousand). The works produced five thousand cycles a year.

The wheel-making department of the Quinton Cycle Co. Ltd, 1896. The factory, in Warwick Road near the station, produced cycles such as the 'Quinton Full Roadster' and the 'Eaton Safety'. This firm was only one of the 248 cycle firms in Coventry between 1870 and 1930.

An advertisement for Singer's Cycles, 1886. The scene reflected reality, for here along the Kenilworth Road and Coat of Arms Bridge Road Coventry cyclists came in their thousands. The bridge bore the crest of the Gregory-Hood family of Styvechale Hall who gave land here for the construction of the railway. During this period Coventry had

dozens of cycling clubs which travelled the highways and byways of leafy Warwickshire every weekend. Many Coventry cycle clubs often outnumbered the inhabitants of the villages they were visiting.

The 'Swift' quadruplet, one of Coventry's more unusual cycles, 1895.

The endurance of the Coventry 'Swift' tandem was proved in 1895 by M. Holbein (left) and J. Bennett who rode this cycle 394½ miles in twenty-four hours, thus creating a world record.

Harry Lawson and his wife in Brighton at the tiller of a German-built Gottlieb-Daimler-engined car in the Emancipation Run, November 1896. The run celebrated the end of the Red Flag Act which restricted the speed of vehicles on British roads, making it virtually impossible to drive a motor car because the act insisted that the vehicle be preceded by a man carrying a red flag. Harry Lawson was a man small in stature but big in ideas. Lawson set up the British Motor Syndicate with Henry Sturmey and B. Van Praagh and spent a fortune trying to corner the industry by buying all the car-related patents he could lay his hands on, including those of the Gottlieb-Daimler engine. Lawson set up the Daimler Co. in January 1896 at Motor Mills in Radford. Here began the British motor car industry and a year later the first Daimlers left the works. During his life as a motor magnate Lawson dealt with millions of pounds, even paying the American Edward Pennington £100,000 for the rights to his dubious vehicles. Later all the foreign patents he had earlier amassed became worthless and in 1904 the founder of the British motor car industry was found guilty of fraud and sentenced to a year's hard labour. He died in 1925, a forgotten man with less than £10 to his name.

Inventor and con-man Edward J. Pennington (top hat) with his sister driving his Pennington Victoria in the Butts in 1896. Pennington, an American from Indiana, left his homeland being pursued for fraud. He arrived in England promoting his inventions and soon made himself known to Harry Lawson who promptly offered him a floor of Motor Mills and the huge sum of £100,000 in cash for his patents. Pennington made unfounded claims for his vehicles, most of which only existed on paper, to draw in other investors. He wore sharp suits and had lavish offices both at Motor Mills and in London. Despite his promises and his many publicity stunts on his autocar Pennington never produced a single vehicle for a private buyer. This, however, did not stop him accepting investments in his company. Soon questions were being asked and one morning Pennington failed to turn up at his office. It was quickly discovered that he had suddenly left the country for America. Within weeks Lawson discovered that Pennington was reselling the patents he had paid for so lavishly, and tried to sue. Meanwhile Pennington tried unsuccessfully to jump on the aeroplane bandwagon and was once again pursued by investors he had conned. Suddenly and unexpectedly Pennington died in 1911 and was buried in a cheap grave. Perhaps this was his last great con.

Motor Mills, Radford, home of Daimler and the Great Horseless Carriage Co., birthplace of the British motor industry. Despite the Daimler Co. being founded by Harry Lawson in January 1896, a year passed before the first British-made motor car left the works. Motor Mills originated as a cotton mill which was gutted by fire on 13 December 1890.

Looking north in Broadgate and down Cross Cheaping, *c.* 1899. This excellent view shows many modes of transport: the horse and cart; horse-drawn hackney carriages (centre); a carriage driven by a liveried chauffeur (right); a motor car (front); and trams (centre background).

Trams in Hales Street at the junctions of Ford Street and Jesson Street, 1899. The Victorian trams of the Coventry Electric Tramway Co. were powered via the movable rod on the roof attached to the criss-cross of cables seen above the roadway. Previously Coventry's trams were steam-powered, noisy and sometimes unreliable. In 1895 the system was electrified and in 1897 a proposal was put before Parliament for an extension to the system from the city down Hales Street, Ford Street and Jesson Street, taking the system into Stoke, Bell Green, the Gosford Green area and Hillfields.

SECTION TWO

Edwardian Times 1900–1910

Coventry's Lady Godiva of 1902, Vera Guedes, poses with attendant next to a rhubarb patch somewhere in the centre of Coventry. This woman from the London Hippodrome carried on the tradition of an actress playing the part, for it was considered unseemly for any ordinary young lady to be seen in such a manner. The 1902 procession marked the coronation of Edward VII.

Hales Street, 1 January 1900. After a night's torrential rain the citizens of Coventry awoke to scenes like this stretching from Pool Meadow to Queen Victoria Road. The water from the flooded River Sherbourne partially refilled the valley which two thousand years earlier had been a real lake. Behind the curious spectators can be seen the Opera House (opened 1889), home of films, plays, musicals, pantos and lectures by many famous individuals, such as George Bernard Shaw, Ernest Shackleton the explorer, and Captain Webb, the first man to swim the Channel. He would have felt very much at home on this particular day! Behind the Opera House stands the grammar school on the corner of Bishop Street. The wall (left) forms the boundary of the Smithfield Market, used until the twentieth century as a cattle market. In the eighteenth century the area in the foreground was a small pool formed by the conflux of the River Sherbourne and Radford Brook.

Edwardian firemen in their full splendour, with brass helmets and steam-powered appliances, outside the Central Fire Station in Hales Street which opened in 1902. It is said that when the fire bell was sounded the horses would dash from their stables at the rear of the station and wait to be put in harness. The Coventry Fire Brigade, one of the first in the country, was formed after 1861 as a volunteer service. Its headquarters were in St Mary's Street. In 1936 the force became fully professional and the cottages on the left of the station were demolished and three more bays added to the station.

Little Butcher Row, which joined Great Butcher Row to Cross Cheaping, 1902. On the right of the man in the doorway is the beginning of the Bull Ring which stood between Priory Row and New Buildings. Here it was ordered that all bulls be baited before slaughtering and in 1565 Queen Elizabeth I was entertained here with one of her favourite sports: badger baiting!

The Smithford Street entrance to Coventry Barracks, 1902. This entrance, built in 1793, bears the GR of George III either side of the gateway. Through this entrance filed horsemen of the Dragoons, Hussars and Lancers. Coventry's permanent garrison became an important part of the city's social life, and military displays were a favourite event in the social calendar. In the 1880s the Royal Field Artillery was stationed here. My own great-grandfather, Charles McGrory, seems to have first brought the McGrorys to Coventry with this regiment, for he was in charge of the horses which pulled the field guns.

Tramcar No. 27 makes its way up Broadgate, 1902. The buildings in the background stand in Cross Cheaping. The fire-ladder behind the cabs was placed here a few years earlier after the death of Mrs Burdett when fire engulfed part of the premises of David Burdett, stationer and printer (mid-background). Note the man drinking water from the fountain in the centre.

Looking up Bishop Street, *c.* 1904. This interesting view shows an entire street which no longer exists. In the seventeenth century there was an area of open ground behind the buildings on the left in which was kept a herd of fallow deer. The white building at the top is eighteenth-century Canal House, which was the administration centre for the nearby canal basin.

A derailment off the Albany Road Bridge, 2 July 1904. To get to the carriages a track was laid down to the road and the carriages dragged back up by a steam-engine. This scene was sold in local shops as a postcard.

Demolition of property in Earl Street, 1905. This was part of the site of Coventry Castle built by warlord Earl Ranulf Gernons in the twelfth century. Caesar's Tower at the back of St Mary's Hall was probably part of the original castle, which after a short and bloody history fell into ruin. This site remained clear until the building of the Council House got underway in 1913. On the right are the police headquarters which opened in 1865.

Derby Lane looking towards The Toby's Head in Pepper Lane, *c.* 1905. Buildings from the sixteenth century line this lane which once ran behind the city gaol. The lane suffered bomb damage in the war and was totally built over when Cathedral Lanes was erected in 1990.

Looking up a narrow High Street, 1906. Practically every building in this view dates from before the seventeenth century. The ancient buildings on the right were swept away when the road was widened in 1928. The Rose and Crown (The Courtyard), hidden from view, is said to have accommodated highwayman Dick Turpin on his ride north.

Half-way up Hertford Street, 1907. On the left under Wilson's Dental Surgery is a Rudge cycle shop selling cycles from the Spon Street works. The large building at the top of this view is the Old Corn Exchange, later the Empire cinema.

The actress Patsy Montagu, whose stage name was 'La Milo', in the role of Lady Godiva, 1907.

Looking north down Butcher Row in 1908. This scene, unchanged for centuries, shows the old drainage channel down the centre of the lane. This channel was said to run with blood on the days the street's butchers had allocated for slaughtering. Rings set into the cobbles were used to draw the animals' heads down with a rope for dispatching. Children often pestered the butchers to let them hold these ropes. Later the slaughter of animals was revolutionized by the hammer-gun invented by Coventry's John Cash.

A view from Warwick Row looking up Hertford Street and Warwick Lane, *c.* 1909. To the left of Christchurch stands The Commercial and Temperance Hotel which previously went under the name of The Birds Hotel. Narrow Warwick Lane and Greyfriars Lane were once the main route into this side of the city and here at the end of Warwick Lane stood the once magnificent Greyfriars Gate, built with local stone given by King Richard II.

The old Cathedral, then the parish church of St Michael, *c.* 1909. This was the largest parish church in England and the third tallest spire in the land. The church was elevated to cathedral status in 1918. When excavations took place in 1891 on the north side of the tower it was found to have been on the edge of a ditch at least 40 ft deep. This is likely to have been part of the Red Ditch, an early defensive ditch actually cut into the bedrock itself. Below the tower the ditch was filled with rubble, old stone coffins and pieces of stonework from a more ancient building. On top of this the north buttress was built and from the time of its construction subsidence has caused the tower to lean, threatening the very structure itself. Stone, concrete and lead has been added in the past to counteract the problem.

The Pilgrims Rest on the corner of Ironmonger Row and Palmer Lane, 1909. The sign above the door informs us that this was built on the site of the original monastic inn in 1820. The inn, like its surroundings, fell to developers in 1936. Medieval pilgrims who followed this lane would have found themselves at the gate which led to the precincts of the Cathedral church and Benedictine priory of St Mary's, one of the richest monastic houses in England. The church, which contained numerous relics, including the arm of St Augustine (originally presented to Coventry's St Osburg's nunnery by King Canute), was the yearly destination of thousands of pilgrims.

SECTION THREE

The First World War Years 1910–1920

The Hendon actress Miss Viola Hamilton was the popular Godiva of 1911. The procession, set to coincide with the coronation of George V, was a huge success, with twenty-three thousand parading schoolchildren and hundreds of individuals dressed as famous historical characters. This was the first time the lady was led by a nun.

Looking down Trinity Lane at the cottage in Priory Row, 1910.

Looking up Trinity Lane (the rear of Butcher Row) from Priory Row, *c.* 1910. On the left is the churchyard of Holy Trinity church.

A fine view of St Michael's from Pepper Lane, *c.* 1910. The inn on the right is The Toby's Head which had been here before 1850. The inn was flattened by a high explosive bomb on 14 November 1940 and two years later a demolition worker uncovered the cellar which still contained twenty barrels of beer. At the bottom of the lane (left) is the County Hall and right is the Golden Cross.

Peeping Tom in the specially constructed fourth-storey window of The King's Head. This postcard, dating from around 1910, is in reality a composite picture. The figure of Tom wearing his tin cockade hat (which he only wore during the Godiva Procession) is from a photograph taken by Coventry chemist Joseph Wingrave in the yard of The King's Head when the figure had been repainted around 1860. This photograph has been placed upon a painting of Tom's nook, commissioned especially some sixty years later, and thus this postcard was created.

The chassis of Daimler cars being test driven around Sandy Lane and St Nicholas Street, Radford, *c.* 1910. The birth of the British motor industry in Radford at Motor Mills must have made quite a noisy impact on the area, for at the time most of Radford was quiet rolling meadows and country lanes.

Butcher Row looking north on a busy day, 1910. To the right of Hilton's Booteries (background) lies Broadgate. This photograph was taken just opposite to the entrance of Priory Row.

Looking down Warwick Row, 1911. Here lived many of Coventry's respectable middle-class traders and business people, including Samuel Vale of watchmaking fame. The last in the row, once called 'Nantglyn', was the school of novelist George Eliot. Here she sat staring out at the open fields while her mind considered higher matters.

Trams going down Broadgate, 1913. The covered tram in front was one of eleven purchased by Coventry Tramways Co. in 1912. The open-top trams in the background continued in service until the Second World War. Astley, advertised on the truck, was the city's oldest firm dating back to 1730. Note the Whitfield's building (left) bears the date of its construction in 1513.

The inner courtyard of the Palace Yard in Earl Street, 1914. Through the arch can be seen the main courtyard and further ahead still the arch leading into Earl Street. A tiny detail there shows wooden scaffolding which marks the first stage of the building of the Council House (begun 1913). It is said that via this courtyard one could walk into Little Palace Yard (demolished 1961) in Little Park Street.

A rare view, from the *Coventry Herald* of October 1914, of the fourteenth-century inner-gateway to Whitefriars monastery which stood near the London Road side of the building. The walk which led from this gate to the monastery was called Bachelor's Walk, probably because all that passed this way in the past were monks. Another explanation is that the gate had a reputation as a place where bachelors brought their sweethearts for a kiss and cuddle in its dark archway. Within the gate were stone seats which were used in the past by the poor who gathered here weekly to receive alms from the brothers of Whitefriars. It is interesting to note the differences between the twentieth-century ground level and the gate's fourteenth-century ground level on this particular site. The inner-gate of Whitefriars was destroyed by a direct hit from a high explosive bomb on 14 November 1940.

A fine Tudor fireplace, illustrating a typical example of Coventry's once hidden past, from the *Coventry Graphic*, 30 January 1914. Buildings in the city centre were often deceiving, appearing to date from Georgian or Victorian times, yet in reality being refaced medieval or Tudor buildings. This photograph was taken at the rear of the premises of Messrs Ralph Smyth & Co. which once stood in the High Street. When Mr Smyth originally moved into the room it had an ordinary fire-grate set into the wall. When the room was being redecorated it was noticed that something seemed to be embedded in the wall. The plaster was carefully chipped away and from it emerged this splendid fire-surround bearing a date of 1565 and the Norman-French legend '*Dieu Done Tout*' meaning 'God Gives All'. The surround was moved to the Drill Hall in the 1930s and later placed in storage when the Hall was demolished.

Looking north down Butcher Row, *c.* 1915. On the left, with a huge pavement display, is the fifteenth-century premises of Franks House Furnishers. Franks stood on the site of the present flower-bed in Trinity Street.

The Great Hall, St Mary's Hall, Bayley Lane, *c.* 1915. Remnants of the city's once large armoury line the minstrels gallery. Here, from the fourteenth to seventeenth century, the city waits played at civic functions.

The north end of St Mary's Great Hall, *c.* 1915. The fifteenth-century tapestry beneath the window (of the same date) shows the marriage of Henry VII to Elizabeth of York, who were regular visitors to the city. The tapestry is bordered by white and red roses showing the marriage uniting the warring houses of Lancaster and York. The painting (right) is a life-size portrait of George III and now hangs in the local museum.

A rather dusty Nave's Post fixed to the wall of the kitchen in St Mary's Hall. Taken from its eighteenth-century wall nook in Much Park Street the figure was placed here in 1900. The blackened late medieval whipping post was originally fixed into the ground and criminals were chained to it and flogged. In 1605 the City Accounts inform us, 'Paid for 2 Padlocks for the Whipping Poste . . . viii d [8d]'. The figure is thought to have originally represented a shackled criminal.

The stocks outside St Mary's Hall (entrance to Castle Yard), *c.* 1905. The Coventry Leet Book lists ten sets of stocks, mainly standing by the city gates. These were in Mill Lane (Cox Street), Bishop Street, Well Street, New Street, Warwick Lane, Little Park Street, Spon Street, Hill Street, Gosford Street and Whitefriars Lane. In the seventeenth century there were also stocks in the Bull Ring (Trinity Street), Vicar Lane, the Market Square and 'by the cage' in Cross Cheaping. The latter was a tall cage on a pivot in which the criminal was incarcerated. Passers-by would spin this contraption to befuddle the prisoner. The stocks shown here originated in the Market Square (site of Hotel Leofric) and were erected here in 1900 and removed in 1929. Before these stocks were removed from the Market Square in 1865 they were frequented many times by two men who both claimed to be 'King of the Stocks'. George 'Trodge' Chittem, a ribbon weaver, when enclosed in the stocks mastered the art of slipping out of them to sup a pint of ale in the nearby Spread Eagle Inn. If asked to go for a drink when a constable was in the watch-house behind the stocks, Chittem would say, 'Don't be a fool, you know I can't come'. His challenger for 'King' was Charlie Kirk, a watchmaker and noted 'tippler'. Kirk spent so much time in these stocks that while in them he continued his daily work as a watch-cock engraver and was often surrounded by a crowd admiring the intricacy and beauty of his work.

On Saturday 18 July 1919, after rain ruined the evening of the Godiva 'Peace' Procession, crowds gathered in Broadgate. Soon The King's Head Hotel, which seems to have had some pre-war German connection, found itself under attack. A large mob fought police in Broadgate with hails of bricks, stones and bottles. The police won the fight but the following evening trouble began again with a window-smashing orgy in Broadgate. The mob were supplied with stones by women who filled their aprons from a building site in Market Square. Eventually the riot was quelled at 2 a.m. Monday night the mob once again gathered smashing windows and now looting. The police (including office staff) were brought to face the mob and ordered to draw truncheons; they attacked the mob, driving them down Cross Cheaping away from the city centre and fighting running battles. For the next few nights Coventry was under curfew and all was quiet. Few knew the reason for the riots, but many believed it was due to anti-German feelings started by rumourmongers among thousands of ex-servicemen, many of whom had returned home for find themselves unemployed. Coventry was not an isolated case, for rioting spread throughout the land in 1919. This photograph was probably taken on Tuesday 21 July when all the smashed shop fronts had been boarded up, and shows Broadgate leading to Salmon & Gluckstein (one of the first shops attacked) which leads into High Street.

A deserted Broadgate, empty due to a curfew, on Tuesday 21 July 1919 at 7.25 p.m. A lone policeman enforces the curfew.

An idyllic Sunday afternoon in Nauls Mill Park, Radford, *c.* 1910. Swans cruise the old mill pool and in the background the band pipes up before a large and appreciative audience. This postcard reflects a scene of Edwardian elegance which sadly died many years ago. Beyond the surrounding hills lies Radford village and miles and miles of open countryside.

SECTION FOUR

The Twenties 1920–1930

The first non-actress to play Godiva was Muriel Mellerup of Gloucestershire, described in the press as the most 'perfect Godiva', who rode in the Coventry Hospital Pageant, 29 June 1929. Miss Mellerup was so popular she remained in the city for some time as guest of the lord and lady mayor. This photograph was taken by E.W. Appleby, a prolific photographer whose work was destroyed in the 1940–1 Blitz.

This unusual view off New Buildings and Hill Top (*c.* 1920) shows the spire of Holy Trinity rising above a building built against the hillside, underneath the garden, between Hill Top and Trinity Street. Legend has it that in this stepped hillside lies a huge cavern in which lived a great dragon who was killed by Coventry's St George. Legend also informs us that under here lie the crypts of St Mary's priory, big enough to drive buses into.

A postcard of Butcher Row in the 1920s, drawn as part of a series of views by Coventry artist Florence Weston who specialized in watercolours and pen and ink. Florence also did the occasional oil painting some of which appear in auction.

The cloisters of Whitefriars monastery, *c.* 1920. The tables and benches were used by the inmates for dining purposes as the ex-monastery became a workhouse in 1801. The ex-workhouse is thought to be haunted by the ghost of an inmate, James Clarke, who hanged himself here in July 1834.

Far Gosford Street, *c.* 1920. On the right is The Hertford Arms next to the Scala cinema. Opposite (by the parked car) can be seen The Pitt's Head, once a meeting place for the prize-fighting fraternity in the early to mid-nineteenth century. One landlord of this inn was John 'Fatty' Adrian (1806–56) who fought a number of bouts before 1850. Adrian became the landlord of The Windmill in Spon Street. Adrian's last two fights were against Bill Betteridge of Nuneaton. The first took place in a field near The Engine public house in Longford in November 1830. Adrian, giving away 7 inches in height and 2 stone in weight fought Betteridge for two and three-quarter hours before the fight was broken up by local constables. As this fight was undecided the two men met again for a £100 purse at Fillongley on 10 April 1831. The Coventry newspapers reported the great excitement surrounding this fight and covered the contest blow by blow. The fight itself lasted over two hours and went for eighty-five rounds (meaning eighty-five knock-downs). From round fifty-seven Betteridge began to come out on top and after a severe beating Adrian's seconds threw in the towel. It is said nearly ten thousand people watched the fight. John Adrian lost his last battle in 1856 while living in Cook Street, when he died from bronchitis and injured ribs, no doubt the results of his earlier career.

The First World War tank which stood on Greyfriars Green behind the statue of Sir Thomas White, *c.* 1922. This 35 ton, 125 horse power tank was placed here on a concrete base in January 1920. It was presented to the city by Major General Sir H.B. Walker on 2 October 1920 from the National War Savings Committee in gratitude for the massive £8½ million raised by the city for the war effort. The tank was produced in the city by the Daimler Company at Drapers Field off Sandy Lane, Radford. The car factory turned out forty of these vehicles a week, thousands of which helped turn the tide of the First World War. The tank had pride of place as a war souvenir until the 1930s when many no longer wished to be reminded of the conflict. The tank was inspected in 1937 by an ex-Daimler tank tester and was found to have its tracks rusted solid; its engine, however, was in perfect condition. When it was removed in 1938 the engine started first time after having lain dormant for eighteen years. The tank was then shunted to remove the rust off the tracks and driven onto a low lorry which took it to its new resting place, opposite the Navigation Bridge on Stoney Stanton Road. It was later scrapped for the war effort during the Second World War.

The old Coventry Hippodrome in Hales Street, *c.* 1923. Note its close proximity to Swanswell Gate. The old Hippodrome was built in 1907 and many a famous name trod its boards until it was demolished in 1937. It is said that even the great Charlie Chaplin appeared here before he left England for America. The old Hippodrome was purchased by Sir Alfred Herbert in May 1936 so that he could extend Lady Herbert's garden, and the new (present) Hippodrome, built nearby, opened on 1 November 1937 at a cost of £100,000. In the shadow of the new building the old Hippodrome was demolished.

A traditional view of Coventry in 1923 showing (left to right) Holy Trinity, St Michael's and Christchurch.

The quadrangle of Bond's Hospital (left) and Bablake School (right), *c.* 1925. The school has open galleries both upstairs and downstairs. The fourth side of the quadrangle was formed by the rear of the city bridewell, a long brick building which housed petty offenders until its closure in 1831.

Looking down the High Street from Broadgate, *c.* 1922. This postcard view issued around 1930 shows High Street Corner 'As it Was' before the right hand side of the street was widened in 1928. The photograph was taken during either the morning or evening rush-hour, when Coventry's cloth-capped multitude wended their way to and from work on locally made cycles. The two buildings on the right stood at the top of Broadgate. From the right they are the National Provincial Bank and the Coventry Arms. Both these buildings were demolished in 1929 for the new columned National Provincial Bank, now the National Westminster. Beneath these façades were hidden buildings dating back to the late medieval period. In ancient times Salmon & Gluckstein and Martins Bank next door were the site of the gateway by which Coventry Castle was entered, the 'Brodeyate' to the Earl of Chester's castle.

Looking down Priory Row to Butcher Row, 1926.

Leicester Street off the top of Bishop Street, 1926. A row of eighteenth-century workers' cottages stands empty, boarded up, as four capped men watch the photographer. Many of Coventry's back streets were once lined with the warm red bricks of cottages such as these. Had these buildings been restored, they would now be considered highly desirable properties.

The junction of Well Street with Bishop Street and the Burges, 1928. At this time Corporation Street (opened 5 July 1931) did not exist. Most of the buildings on the left were demolished between 1930 and 1931 to make way for the new street.

Looking up Greyfriars Lane, 1928. Ford's Hospital (founded 1509, right) took a direct hit from a bomb in October 1940 and the damaged section was explored by city historian John Bailey Shelton. Shelton dug below the matron's room and found remains of a fourteenth-century floor covered with decorated encaustic tiles. One tile bore the black eagle of Earl Leofric and formed part of what was thought to be the floor of a chapel or similar building, probably connected to the nearby Greyfriars monastery which took up much of the surrounding land. In the last century labourers laying drains a few yards down the lane unearthed a large number of golden crowns dating from the reign of Henry VIII. Buried in 'rubbishy material' the coins were 'perfectly bright and clean' as the day they were buried.

SECTION FIVE

The Thirties 1930–1940

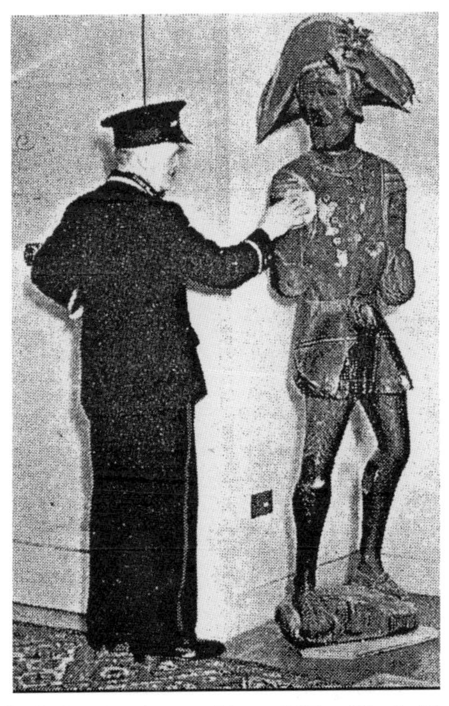

Peeping Tom with cockade hat in the corridor of The King's Head, 1934. The figure was removed from its special nook on the fourth floor; the intention was to cast a head and shoulder image as a replacement for the original, which was to be kept indoors, but this was never carried out.

A fine image of Peeping Tom placed in the window of a timbered house in Bishop Street, created by local sculptor T. Freeman, *c.* 1930. The figure, like the house, is now gone.

An image of Peeping Tom (*c.* 1930) based on the original in The King's Head (now in Cathedral Lanes), but this time peeping from a corner of the Peeping Tom Hotel at the bottom of Hertford Street. This figure, which seems to date from the late nineteenth century, can now be seen in the entrance to the covered way at the top of the street.

A view taken from the nave, looking down the chancel and aspe of St Michael's, *c.* 1931. The nave measures 37 ft 6 in across, making it one of the widest in England. The two figures in the piers are of St Peter and St Paul and were placed there in 1861. The three windows seen in the apse contain a stained-glass memorial to Queen Adelaide which dates from 1853. The remaining two windows, either side of the apse, contained much of the building's finest remaining medieval glass, including the work of Coventry's famous John Thornton. This glass was removed before the Second World War and stored at Hampton Lucy. What remains is now scattered in various places.

Looking from the north aisle in front of the tomb of Julian Nethermyl towards the south-west door in the south aisle, *c.* 1931. The font is thought to have been the one presented to the church by John Cross, mayor in 1394, as it bore a brass plaque bearing what was thought to be his merchant mark. The light beyond the font comes from the open Great West Door. On the left, under the arches, was the Dyers chapel, established by the Dyers Company when Coventry was a centre of the wool and dyeing trade which gave Coventry its famous 'As true as Coventry Blue' dye.

Looking across the nave into the north aisle and the Girdlers and St Andrews chapels, 1931. The Girdlers chapel was founded in 1390 and mass was sung here before an altar dedicated to All Saints. St Andrews or the Smiths chapel was founded by the Smiths Company around 1449. These chapels, however, are later versions as the aisle was not built until after 1500. The Nethermyl tomb in relation to this view would be on the far left, at the end of the north aisle.

A fine brass eagle lectern (*c.* 1931) standing at the base of the pillar which divides the nave from the bottom of the north aisle, behind which stood the Lady chapel (and the present entrance from the new Cathedral made from a window). This fine piece of ecclesiastical furniture was created by F.A. Skidmore in 1867 and bore this inscription on the base: 'To the glory of God and for the use of St. Michael's Church, Coventry. This lectern has been placed in this chancel from a legacy by the late John Royle, Solicitor of this city. MDCCCLXVII [1867] who died November 9th 1866 aged 60.' Behind in the chancel can be seen part of the rows of fifteenth-century choir stalls which held below their seats fine carved misericords depicting religious and mythical scenes and images. Hidden within the pillar behind the lectern was a spiral stairwell which once led to the top of medieval carved-oak rood-screen which once separated the people from the clergy.

A fine view of the three spires, *c.* 1932. The Crimean cannon stands among a well-pruned and finely trimmed Greyfriars Green.

Warwick Row and Greyfriars Green, *c.* 1932. The railed area behind Sir Thomas White's statue holds the First World War tank which resided here for eighteen years.

Palace Yard, Earl Street, *c.* 1932. The fifteenth-century mansion of the Hopkins family entertained the Princess Elizabeth (later Queen of Bohemia) (1605), the Duke of Monmouth (1682), James II (1687) and the Princess (later Queen) Anne (1688). The 'Yard' went through various guises. In the eighteenth century it was a coaching inn with fine rooms and stabling in the inner courtyard. A bottle found in 1937, hidden in a column at the inn in 1784 by Alderman Thomas Lander Smith, held a piece of paper which informed us in verse that the yard, as an inn, had 'The good Brown Ale our flowing cellars yield; And Rare Sir Loins that oft' our tables Crown [a pun on the inn's name]; Now all the Cheer this Gen'rous house affords.' Later in the nineteenth century the inn became a builder's yard, ribbon warehouse and suchlike, and generally began to fall into disrepair. By 1915 things began to improve when Winifred King used the building as a studio for making fine hand-crafted jewellery and silverwork. The studio expanded when a craft shop was opened to the public in 1927. During its period as a craft house the building was meticulously restored to its former glory, until that fateful night of 14 November 1940 when a massive bomb struck leaving 'only a shapeless heap of debris remaining'. So ended one of Coventry's finest buildings.

A busy view of the Burges, 1932. This scene remains recognizable today with the clock (right) still ticking away. There are no buses stopping here, as now, but trams go to and fro to Broadgate picking up fares. To the left of the workmen is a gap between the buildings in which could be found a small ancient sandstone bridge which straddled the River Sherbourne. Two thousand years earlier this view would have shown the narrowest section of a huge lake which filled the central valley of the site of Coventry. Here (between Silver Street and Palmer Lane) a Roman legion, probably led by Agricola (who, legend states, built a camp on Barrs Hill), built a 200 yd long wooden causeway across the lake. The high ground either side of this long-gone construction has produced coins and pottery fragments dating back to the reigns of Nero and Augustus. Higher up in Cross Cheaping a marble statuette of the Roman god of war, Mars, was unearthed in the last century. Interestingly, Mars was one of the gods most favoured by the Roman legions.

St Catherine's Well in Beaumont Crescent, off the Holyhead Road, from the *Coventry Standard*, 1933. Of its known history the well is said to have been a conduit which supplied part of Spon End with water. It gave the surrounding area in Coundon and Radford the name Conduit Fields. From here down to Cramper's Field the Coventry Races were held from 1852 on a course which was described as one of the finest mile circuits in the land. Victorian England's most famous jockey, Fred Archer, won the Packington Plate here in 1874. The chapel-like structure built over the well is thought to date back to the beginning of the 1400s. This structure tells of the well's real origin, for the chapel above it, like many others around the country, shows that the well was originally a holy well. Its water supply must later have been conduited when its religious significance fell from use. Once standing on a grassy knoll within open countryside about a mile or so from Coventry, the well, like most holy wells, probably pre-dates Christianity and was re-dedicated by the Church. St Catherine herself began life as a pagan deity and her wheel was a symbol of the sun. Other traditions connected with the well, concerning an underground cavern or passage, come straight from the pre-Christian belief that these sacred wells were entrances to the underworld. The photograph shows workmen on the then new housing estate, tidying up the site and adding a low stone wall around the structure. It was noted at the time that the foundations of a small, rectangular stone structure lay nearby.

Christchurch, 1933. Originally called Greyfriars and belonging to the Greyfriars (Franciscans), the church was erected after the order came to the city around 1234. Their church and friary were built on land given to the order by Ranulf, Earl of Chester, before his death in 1232. The order proved popular with Coventrians and existed here within their cloistered walls until the Dissolution led to the repression of the order in 1539. The surviving steeple stood alone until the church was rebuilt in early decorated style between 1829 and 1832. This second body was destroyed in a raid in 1941 and the church was later relocated at Cheylesmore.

Looking up Hertford Street and Warwick Lane, 1933. From right to left can be seen Len Cooper's, newsagent and tobacconist; also the offices of G.L. Jackson & Co., tour agents, colliery agents and ticket office for the LMSR (London to Manchester Steam Railway). Above can be seen the tower of Central Hall and across Warwick Lane stands Curtis and Beamish, then Hertford Street over to the Peeping Tom pub.

Hertford Street and Warwick Lane, *c.* 1933. To the left of the Peeping Tom is the entrance to the Barracks Market and car park. It was through this exit, from the then Black Bull Inn, that Lord Northampton escaped after trying to raise men for the king in the Civil War.

Looking up Cross Cheaping from the Burges on a bright morning, 1933. The buildings on the left were to be demolished in 1936 and the first Owen Owen store built on the site. On the corner of Ironmonger Row stands the Board Vaults public house.

Looking down Market Street from Broadgate, 1933. The Market Hall with its tower was opened on the site of the city's ancient market place on 2 December 1867. On the left is Boots the Chemist whose premises took in the corner of Broadgate. Behind Boots is Blackham and Son, opticians, and Bythes, fishmonger. The market building under the tower began life in 1867 as Mary Ann Laxon and Sons, cheese and bacon factors. In the 1930s it was W.C. Smith's Bacon Shop. The market clock reads fourteen minutes to three and no doubt that was exactly right as this clock, created by Edward Loseby, was considered one of the most accurate in the land.

The interior of St Michael's Cathedral, 1935. In the past it was often recorded that the interior of the Cathedral was troubled by birds and bats. Various vicars combated the problem by various means: more than one chose the musket, and the ceiling was studded with bullet holes; another chose a crossbow, firing blunt bolts. In 1687 James II 'touched' three hundred people here to cure scrofula, known as the 'king's evil'.

A busy scene in Little Butcher Row on a sunny afternoon in 1935 looking towards the middle of Cross Cheaping.

Butcher Row from the junction with Priory Row (left) on a wet morning in November 1935. On both sides can be seen C. Jacobs, house furnisher, which held Nos 10, 11 and 18a Butcher Row. The timbered building Nos 7 and 9 was the shop of A.W. Garlick, sheet metal worker, from around 1900. The whole street at that time was awaiting closure and demolition.

Priory Row from Butcher Row, *c.* 1935. Many will recognize the seventeenth-century cottages at the entrance to Priory Row, which survive to this day.

The War Memorial Park, *c.* 1935. Originally belonging to Styvechale Hall, this was opened in July 1921. The park had a fine set of gardens, lovingly tended by a group of park-keepers. Here we see part of the rock gardens.

Another view showing the memorial (dedicated 1927) from the rock gardens, *c.* 1935. Successive Council cutbacks saw these lovely gardens sadly disappear.

A fine view of Lady Herbert's garden, *c.* 1938. The garden was built by Sir Alfred Herbert in memory of his second wife, Florence. The garden on the left was laid out in 1934. The other half, which lay on the other side of the city wall, was created when Swanswell Gate (built 1461) was restored in 1931 and 1932. The bronze railings which surround the garden carry Florence Herbert's initials upon every upright. The dwellings (top and left) were also paid for by Sir Alfred for perpetual use as almshouses. On the Gate itself can be seen remains of the city wall and the blocked doorway which once led on to its parapet.

Work nears completion in 1936 as the fire station in Hales Street is extended with three new bays copied exactly from the original 1902 building.

An interesting view from the tower of Holy Trinity church (early 1936) showing the beginning of demolition work underway on Butcher Row and Cross Cheaping. The work would prove difficult due to the numerous cellars under the buildings which dated from the fifteenth to eighteenth centuries. To understand this view one must remember that Butcher Row in the foreground followed the line of the present flower-bed in Trinity Street. The road running left to right is Broadgate, Cross Cheaping and the Burges. Market Street runs to the Market Tower, and further down West Orchard runs to the bottom of Smithford Street.

The Gulson Library, later Central Library, opposite Holy Trinity, 1936. When the library opened in 1873 as the Free Library, seventeen thousand books were transferred here from the old library in Hertford Street, which was closed in 1868. Samuel Carter gave £1,000 and John Gulson a further £2,000 to build this library which by 1890 contained over eighty thousand books.

Smithford Street, 1936. On the left is Woolworths and next door is the City 'Drinkwater' Arcade (which led to the Barracks Market), built on the original entrance to the barracks. Both were erected back from the original street level. The Council's intention over the following five years was to demolish the whole of the street and rebuild on a line with these buildings.

Looking to the north from the tower of St Michael's, 1936. Noticeable is the amount of industrial chimneys a short distance from the city centre. Despite this, writers of the period who visited the city often expressed surprise that such an industrial centre had such good air quality. The cleared ground in the centre is the area designated for the building of Trinity Street. The lawn behind the buildings in the foreground (Priory Row) was part of the central nave of the great priory church of St Mary four hundred years earlier.

This amazing view shows the area between Butcher Row and Cross Cheaping under demolition for Trinity Street, 1936. Two men stand in front of the entrance to Priory Row, and Holy Trinity dominates the scene of devastation. The construction was held up by the numerous old cellars which littered the site. Also many ancient objects were discovered (and destroyed) during the work.

Looking down Cow Lane from Little Park Street, 1936. It is said that the lane got its name from the fact that herds of cows were driven daily down here until the nineteenth century to graze in the Great Park. The lane was widened in 1927 and the remaining buildings, which date from the fifteenth century, were demolished in the 1930s and '50s.

The Council House on the night of the coronation of George VI, 12 May 1937. The city spent £20,000 on decorations for the great day which began with a procession of 2,500 schoolchildren. Festivities were held all over the city and the children of Coventry received either a commemorative mug or medal. Parties were held throughout the city and dinners were laid on for the elderly at the Drill Hall, Queen Victoria Road, and at the canteen of Alfred Herbert's. Official civic celebrations began at the War Memorial Park at midday and were supposed to end at night with a spectacular firework display. The display ended as a damp squib when the heavens opened up driving everyone home.

Looking from Hertford Street into Broadgate, 1937. Below Hilton's Booteries can be seen Butcher Row in the latter stage of its demolition. James Walker Ltd, jewellers, occupies part of the National Provincial Bank, and above Salmon & Gluckstein, tobacconists, can be seen the spire of Holy Trinity.

Broadgate decorated for the coronation of George VI, 12 May 1937. Many of the city's streets were similarly adorned at a cost of £20,000. The loaded truck (far left) can be seen leaving the fenced-off area as Trinity Street nears completion.

Part of the opening ceremony of Trinity Street, Thursday 16 September 1937. On the stand Mayor Alderman Barnacle addresses the crowd prior to the tape-cutting ceremony. The 'Keep Left' sign in the foreground stands on the site of the 'Vaults' which led into Butcher Row.

A policeman directing night-time traffic at 'Dunn's Corner' before The King's Head on the corner of Hertford and Smithford Street, 1937.

Trams passing from Hertford Street into Broadgate at night, early 1937. The gentleman who took these night-time shots, Mr James Armer, got these pictures by simply asking the trams to stop.

The Cheylesmore Inn, opposite Ford's Hospital, standing on the corner of Warwick Lane and Greyfriars Lane, 1937. The inn was run by Arthur Edward Haymes and occupied the site of an ancient building, probably within the grounds of the Greyfriars monastery, and can be seen marked on Speed's map of the city dated 1610. In 1850 the inn was known as The Bell and was run by a woman called Elizabeth Jephcott.

The view from the roof of the gas showrooms (now the site of Axa-Equity and Law) shows Corporation Street, six years after its construction, looking towards St John's in Fleet Street, 1937. On the right is Fretton Street, now Upper Well Street, where the *Coventry Evening Telegraph* offices stand. On the left is the newly opened (February 1937) Rex cinema showing *The General Died at Dawn*. Sadly Coventry's newest and most lavish cinema, built in the art deco style, was hit by bombs on 25 August 1940. Damage, however, was limited and there was talk of the building's restoration. The cinema was soon showing films again, despite the damage, but this ended on 14 November 1940 when the cinema was entirely destroyed.

Broadgate looking south towards the National Provincial Bank (now the National Westminster Bank), 1937. Note the tram coming up Hertford Street; this year would see the last tram to travel up this particular street as the Council began to phase out the service.

Hertford Street, *c.* 1937. From the top (right) can be seen the Bank Chambers and the post office. Below lies the Queen's Hotel, the city's finest small hotel.

The Starley Memorial in Queens Grove at the end of Warwick Row, 1937. Above the head of James Starley, 'Father of the Cycle Industry', stands the figure of Fame. One hand rests on an anchor, symbolizing renewed hope in Coventry's future. The city had prospered due to Starley's introduction of cycle manufacturing here after the collapse of ribbon weaving in 1861. The industry assured Coventry's future for the next hundred years, for many cycle manufacturers later became makers of motor cars. Starley invented the differential gear found in all modern motor vehicles after losing control of his 'Wonder' cycle while riding up Knightlow Hill. After crawling out of a ditch full of stinging nettles, Starley rubbed dock leaves on his stings, while on a scrap of paper he made a rough sketch with a pencil of the solution to his problem.

Looking down Broadgate into Cross Cheaping and the Burges (left) and Trinity Street (right), 1937. Coventry's new premier department store, Owen Owen, was newly opened and boasted a huge range of quality goods. Little did the builders realize that three years later the store would be no more. The Daimler bus is on its way to the Allesley Old Road.

This fine view shows a spotless Trinity Street a year after its official opening in 1937. On the right are the bus stops to the station, Earlsdon and Baginton. These stand on the site of C. Jacobs, house furnisher, in Butcher Row. The open ground behind was the site of the Bull Ring and the Spotted Dog Inn. The new shops in the lower part of the street are shown nearing completion but still contain no shop fronts. Opposite the Bovis sign marks the site of more shops and later the present Sainsbury's. The Owen Owen store (left) was opened in September 1937.

Cross Cheaping and the Burges, 1937. The left hand side had changed little since the 1860s. K Shoes was a fifteenth-century building; England Shoes, an early eighteenth-century building refaced, followed by George Mason's and Franks, which was a fine fifteenth-century building. Matterson and Huxley was housed in a mid-Victorian building, and buildings beyond date from between 1910 and the 1930s. On the right is the first Owen Owen store.

This view looking down Cuckoo Lane towards Priory Row has changed little since 1938. The massive Priory Cathedral of St Mary's, whose front began by Trinity Street, ended at the far right of this picture. Also to the right once stood the palace of the medieval bishops of Coventry.

Central Methodist Hall at the bottom of Warwick Lane, 1938. The hall replaced a much smaller Wesleyan meeting place which stood nearby. The Methodist movement began in Coventry in the late eighteenth century after three visits to the city by its founder, John Wesley. All the ground in this photograph once belonged to Greyfriars monastery.

Warwick Lane, 1938. In the background stands Central Hall and workmen dig outside G.L. Jackson & Co., tour agent; F. Simons, grocer; B.L. Cramp, tobacconist; the Grapes Inn; and lastly a sports car specialist.

Looking down a deserted High Street towards Broadgate, 1939. Note the bank on the distant left, next to which The King's Head (jutting out) can be seen.

Holy Trinity and St Michael's from the Owen Owen building, 1939. The Trinity Street flower-bed is under construction, as is the mock-Tudor building on the corner. Ironically the building which was to become Timothy White's, chemist, was built on the site of a real Tudor building. Beneath the flower-bed and pavement lie medieval cellars.

A fine view of the High Street from The King's Head on the corner of Hertford Street and Smithford Street, 1939. The familiar National Provincial Bank (National Westminster) stands on the right and on the left, coming around the corner of Broadgate, can be seen Salmon & Gluckstein, the Glove Shop, Martins Bank and Harrison's. All of these buildings are now gone, down to the double-roofed Elizabethan building which had been restored in 1935. It is noticeable that no tram-lines can be seen in the High Street and it never appeared to be used by trams. It was, however, served by buses like the single-decker bus seen here picking up fares.

Looking from the tower of St Michael's at Holy Trinity and beyond, 1938. The new Owen Owen had been trading for a year, and further down the new shops in lower Trinity Street near completion. To the right of Trinity, poking through the trees, is the Bell Campanile which held the bells of Trinity until the 1960s. The four-storey factory block (background left) known as the Victoria Works or 'Paddy's Hart' was built in 1860 by Irishman James Hart of Copsewood Grange. Unfortunately the ribbon weaving mill was completed just as the ribbon trade collapsed. It soon became known as 'Paddy's Folly' but still continued for a short time, producing quality ribbons which were exhibited and won awards at the International Exhibition in London in 1862. Hart's investment in these works proved his downfall; they soon closed and he was forced to sell them and his home. Later the mill came into the hands of the Rover and Centaur companies. Rover held the first, third and fourth floors and the Centaur Company the second floor. Here they rented their steam power from Rover who maintained the steam-engine.

Broadgate from the steps of the National Provincial Bank (now the National Westminster), 1939.

Looking down Warwick Lane, 1939. The building at the bottom of the lane actually stands in Greyfriars Lane next to Ford's Hospital. It was once the home of the *Coventry Standard* newspaper and later the GPO sorting offices.

The choir of St Michael's a year before its destruction, 1939. The tower of the Cathedral is to the left of the window on the left.

The east side of Broadgate, with a policeman directing traffic into the High Street near the entrance of Hertford Street, 1939. The tram, the No. 5, is on its way to the railway station.

Broadgate at 2.40 p.m. from a window in Greyfriars Lane, ten minutes after an IRA bomb exploded, 25 August 1939. The 5 lb bomb placed in the front basket of a cycle was left outside Astley's (near Burtons) and exploded killing three people, a man in his eighties, a 15-year-old boy and a 21-year-old woman making final preparations for her marriage. Many others were injured as pieces of metal shot hundreds of yards through the air. This was the last of many bombs which had shaken the city centre since June. Five people were arrested in connection with the bombings and put on trial. Three were found not guilty; two were found guilty and sentenced to death.

The morning rush-hour in Broadgate and Hertford Street, 1939. The bank dominates the background as traffic pours down the streets. Both trams, Nos 58 and 69, were purchased in 1931 and ran until 1940 to Bell Green and Stoke. The Keresley bus, the 16A, ran from this point to the Shepherd and Shepherdess every fifteen minutes. This

particular vehicle, No. 225, was purchased by Coventry Transport in March 1939. The headline on the news-stand (far right) refers to the recent IRA bombings with 'Lords Rush Through IRA Bill'. Soon the headlines would be 'War'.

The corner of Broadgate and High Street, 1939. On the right are the well-known pillars of the bank and continuing across Greyfriars Lane can be seen Lloyds Bank, Waters and the Craven Arms.

An interesting view from the second-storey window of the City Arcade in Smithford Street on a busy Saturday afternoon, 1939. Note British Home Stores, built back from the original street level following the 1936 plan to rebuild the street. Note also the ARP Shelter signs.

The fine, fourteenth-century wayfarers' chapel of St James and St Christopher by Spon Bridge in Spon Street, 1939. This excellent medieval chapel, used by travellers who could not enter the city when the gates were closed, suffered minor damage in the Blitz and was later reduced to a ruin by the City Council.

Demolition of part of Union Street, *c.* 1939. The remains of the buildings in the street show they date from the fifteenth to eighteenth centuries. In the background can be seen Cow Lane chapel which was once attended by George Eliot and is the meeting house in her novel *Felix Holt*. The minister of the chapel, the Revd Francis Franklin, was the father of her teachers and gave her the character Rufus Lyon.

No. 11 Priory Row in the 1930s. This fine, early eighteenth-century town house, known as Gorton House, was home in the past to many professional gentlemen. In the 1930s it was home to the Coventry Benevolent Burial Collecting Society and the Priory Assembly Rooms. The building was badly damaged in the Blitz, but was later carefully restored. The fine railings are original.

The morning rush-hour in Broadgate from the first floor of the Owen Owen building, 1939. A van belonging to W.R. Fletcher Ltd, butcher, turns across the front of Owen's into Trinity Street. A.D. Wimbush and Boots (right) stand either side of Market Street.

SECTION SIX

The Years of Destruction 1940–1950

Coventrians carrying water (due to burst mains) pass Judges Court in Much Park Street. This photograph was probably taken after one of the April raids in 1940, since the buildings in the background were destroyed in November; by then nearly all Coventrians had to collect their water in this manner due to smashed water mains.

The east side of Broadgate, 1940. War restrictions call for all vehicles to have hoods placed over their headlights. In the background can be seen (left to right): Whitfields, Flinn & Co., Hayward and Sons, Broadgate Café, Newton's, and J. Lyon's café and cake shop. Below the clock the white electrical box carrys posters 'Calling Out Army Reserves'.

Judges Court in Much Park Street, *c.* 1940. The court was used up until the mid-nineteenth century as a residence for visiting circuit judges on the bench of the Coventry assizes. During this period it was used as offices for Dr Phillips, the Tennred Spring Company and McKenna's Light Transport. The buildings, which probably date from the seventeenth century, were partially destroyed in the Blitz.

The mid-fifteenth-century Council Chamber in St Mary's Hall in the 1940s. The chamber was restored to its present condition in 1930. The Jacobean oak panelling came from The Coventry Arms (demolished 1929) which stood on the site of the National Westminster Bank in Broadgate. The ceiling was restored and the carvings, including the central figure of God, restored to their original setting. The tapestry which runs around the wall was designed by MacDonald Gill and woven by the Morris Art Workers at Merton Abbey. It shows (from right of door): the seal of Coventry St Mary's priory; the eagle of Earl Leofric; the wheat sheaves of the Earls of Chester; the three feathers of the Black Prince; and coats of arms of various monarchs associated with the city, including Richard II and Charles I. The furniture around the room from left to right is the Muniment or Treasure Chest, a thirteenth-century chest from Caesar's Tower placed here until the tower was fully rebuilt (1946–9). The Guild Chair dates from around 1450 and may have been used by past mayors and masters of Trinity Guild. The chairs both bear the Elephant and Castle and date from the mid-seventeenth century. The chest is seventeenth century and the figure of St George and the dragon probably dates from the fifteenth century and came from St George's chapel in Gosford Street, which was demolished in the nineteenth century. The refectory table in the centre once belonged to the Lucys of Charlecote Hall.

The crypt of St Mary's Hall (*c.* 1940) showing various old Coventry cycles which were stored here before the city had a proper museum. In the past the crypt was used for storing food, gunpowder and arms in the Civil War, and statues from the tower of St Michael's. At one point within the last hundred years the crypt contained rubbish to a depth of 3 ft.

The smaller raids leading up to 14 November 1940 gave the services valuable experience of what was to come. This raid, which left a crater in Well Street, took place in August 1940. That night's bombing resulted in two houses being destroyed, a dozen damaged and no casualties. Many curious Coventrians came to see, in their words, 'what Jerry had done'.

Morning in Little Park Street, 15 November 1940. People wander the streets of devastated Coventry after eleven long hours of bombing. The previous night began like any other; the sky was clear and a full moon shone down lighting up the rooftops. The bomber squadrons of General Field Marshals Kesselring and Sperrle, numbering over four hundred planes, were following three radio signals which converged on their target: Coventry. Just before 7 p.m. the sirens sounded and a drone could be heard in the air. Twenty minutes passed and the city's ack-ack guns opened up as flares on parachutes hung above the city. Incendiaries began to fall in the centre from the first bombers which were marking the targets. Fires were reported to the fire service as the incendiaries continued falling with their characteristic swishing sound. Ten minutes later the centre began to explode and tremble as high explosives screamed down. A bomber unleased its load every thirty seconds and the pilots could soon smell Coventry burning 1,000 ft below them. Soon the bombers had no need to follow the radio signal for the blazing city could be seen over 150 miles away. Soon two hundred fires were reported and communications broke down as more fires converged, swept across the city by a westerly wind. Streets began to be dynamited to make fire breaks, the city's heart was burnt and ripped apart, leaving 554 dead and 865 injured. In this view the street has been blocked off because an unexploded bomb (one of 280) lay nearby.

The morning of 15 November 1940; the tower and spire of Holy Trinity rises up in the gloom, while Broadgate lies in ruins.

The devastated centre looking across Smithford Street to the Market Clock Tower, 15 November 1940. The night before, this view was said by one man to resemble Dante's *Inferno*.

The ruins of St Michael's looking towards the tower, 15 November 1940. Note the long metal strips in the foreground; these were reinforcements added to the main oak roof-beams during the Cathedral's restoration between 1885 and 1890.

The interior of St Michael's, probably 17 November 1940. The central area has been cleared and people still wander the ruins. Underneath the rubble lie the remains of richly decorated tombs dating back to medieval times. One such tomb was the

Swillington tomb which bore the effigy of a knight in armour and his two wives lying on top, hands clasped in prayer.

This photograph, taken for the *Daily Mirror* on the morning of 15 November 1940, shows the interior of St Michael's shrouded in smoke and full of rubble. In the middle of the Cathedral can be seen what looks like crossed burnt timbers. These are in fact strips of metal which were used to reinforce the main roof-beams in the 1885–90 restoration. This image gave rise to the story of the charred cross, which in reality was spontaneously created by the Cathedral's stonemason, Jack Forbes. It is interesting to note that the buildings behind the Cathedral seem basically intact; these would suffer in later raids in April 1941. St Michael's was destroyed by a string of incendiary bombs which set fire to the inner roof space after burning through the lead roof. As the Cathedral burned, most thought it safe, for the bells continued to strike the hour.

Looking across Broadgate towards the Market Tower from the lane leading to Holy Trinity church, 15 November 1940. The burnt-out shop on the left was erected just two years earlier.

Looking from Hertford Street into Broadgate, 15 November 1940. The east side of Broadgate lies in smouldering ruins as Martins Bank (right) stands untouched. On the left is Burtons on the corner of Smithford Street.

The remains of a Riley Kestrel parked outside the ruins of Boots the Chemist in Broadgate on the morning of 15 November 1940. Surprisingly the vehicle is still running to this day, as it was taken back to the Riley works and restored.

Looking down Cross Cheaping from Owen Owen, the morning of 15 November 1940. To the left of the man carrying the suitcase is Market Street. Much of the debris on the right consists of metal window frames which fell from the store's windows as they buckled in the intense heat.

A soldier on duty in the smouldering ruins of Jordan Well (in front of the present museum), 15 November 1940. Behind can be seen the tower of the Council House and the spire of St Michael's. Shovels can be seen lying by the roadside as the roads, once impassable, were slowly cleared.

This shows the force of some of the explosions which rocked the city on the night of 14 November 1940. Here we have an ambulance which was sent hurtling through the air onto this balcony at the Coventry and Warwickshire Hospital.

Two fire wardens casually glance at a car which has crashed into a bomb crater killing the driver in Much Park Street by Whitefriars Gate, 16 November 1940. To the right can be seen the Coach and Horses, an inn which was here in the mid-eighteenth century when the street was the venue for horse fairs. Nothing except the Gate survived into the late 1960s.

Vicar Lane, once known as Hounds Lane, 16 November 1940. The rubble around the lamp-post is in Smithford Street, and beyond leading to the Market Tower is Market Street. In 1611, when the lane was an open square, a set of stocks was set up here mainly to punish insanitary waste dumpers. Vicar Lane once held the non-conformist chapel led by the noted nineteenth-century cleric, Revd John Sibree. The lane backed onto the barracks and every Sunday the regimental band entertained visitors until Sibree complained and thereby stopped the practice.

The shell of Owen Owen and the burnt-out Market Hall amid a tangle of buildings destroyed by high explosives, 17 November 1940. The roads are clear and at the top of Cross Cheaping work begins on the gigantic task of removing the rubble which was once the city of Coventry. Owen Owen had already suffered during an earlier raid when it was hit by a single, heavy high explosive which plunged through the roof and two floors before exploding on the ground floor. The building was to be restored until it was dealt the death blow by a string of incendiaries on 14 November.

High Street lies in ruins as a Ministry of Information van travels the city advising survivors on food and water supplies, 16 November 1940. Most food supplies were destroyed and the water system extensively damaged and polluted by burst sewerage pipes.

Less than twenty-four hours after the 'Big Raid' the city still smoulders as soldiers search for bodies among the rubble which only hours earlier was the top of Cross Cheaping, 15 November 1940.

Looking down Cross Cheaping from the bottom of Broadgate on the morning of 15 November 1940. People wander the city to talk about and view the destruction. On the right stands the remains of Owen Owen, and on the left the burnt-out shell of a Corporation bus, one of half of the city's fleet to be destroyed.

Jordan Well at midday, 15 November 1940. Soldiers were drafted into the city to keep order and help search for those missing, many of whom lay dead or injured, buried in the rubble. The centre of the road had been cleared, unlike some roads like nearby Bailey Lane which was filled with rubble 4 ft deep.

The mass burial of the victims of the 'Big Raid' of 14 November 1940, on 20 November 1940. The grave consisted of two long trenches holding simple oak coffins, two deep. Thousands gathered at the London Road Cemetery as sermons were given by clergy of different denominations. After the sermons were read the lord mayor led the mourners to the graveside and many searched in vain for their loved ones as clergymen moved among them offering solace. Amid the sounds of sobbing a Merlin engine was heard purring in the distance as a Spitfire saluted the dead with a victory roll in the clear November sky.

A wing of the Coventry and Warwickshire Hospital being cleared after a raid, April 1941. The old hospital was almost totally destroyed after suffering direct hits from bombs and incendiaries. The heavy raid resulted in the deaths of two doctors, nine nurses, two porters and twenty patients. Four members of staff were awarded George Medals.

The partially cleared interior of Christchurch, late 1941. The tower dates from the fourteenth century and the body of the church from 1832. Beneath the arch was the altar; this was smashed when the church bell fell from the belfry above. The building was burnt out by incendiaries on 8 April 1941. The walls were demolished in 1950 and the spire once again stands alone for the second time in its history.

The interior of the old grammar school in Hales Street (1941), originally the fourteenth-century church of the Hospital of St John, which was founded in the twelfth century to aid the sick, poor and wayfarers. It fell into the hands of the Crown in 1539 when Henry VIII dissolved the monasteries, and was then acquired by John Hales, who turned it into a grammar school in 1557 and furnished it with carved choir stalls from the fourteenth-century church of Whitefriars. It served as a school until 1885, educating such people as Sir William Dugdale, historian, Dr Philemon Holland, the 'translator general' of many classics, and Michael Drayton, noted sixteenth-century poet. Queen Elizabeth I visited Coventry in August 1565. Entering the city via Bishop Street she stopped at the school to view the building's fine library and presented money to the master of the house for its upkeep. The building has been badly neglected throughout the twentieth century.

The visit of King George VI and Queen Elizabeth to the ruins of St Michael's, 25 February 1942. Talking to the King is the bishop, Dr Mervyn Haigh, and with the Queen, St Michael's Revd R.T. Howard. In the centre (behind) can be seen the mayor, Alderman Moseley.

Looking south from Owen Owen across West Orchard, 1942. All the ruins have been cleared leaving wide-open empty spaces. The right corner of this photograph was once the site of the Market Hall with Market Street running from the left, across and turning into Smithford Street, which runs left to right across the view. On the left (background) stands the Empire cinema and the spire of Christchurch.

A fascinating view of the city centre from the tower of St Michael's, 1942. In the foreground can be seen the edge of Holy Trinity with a ladder for use during raids leaning against its side. Next to it stands the untouched section of the Central Library which survived the 'Big Raid'. Broadgate is completely gone except for Burtons (left) on the corner of Smithford Street, which can be seen leading down to St John's. In the centre, in Market Street, stands the Market Clock Tower, once attached to the Market Hall which opened in 1867. A week before the tower was demolished in December 1942 a young boy was killed by falling masonry. The night before its demolition Samuel Corbett died, aged eighty-seven years old. He had been custodian of the clock, winding it up every week since 1892. Right of the tower is West Orchard leading down from the bottom of Smithford Street and into Cross Cheaping, in which stands Owen Owen, gutted and advertising 'War Savings'. In the background (mid-right) can be seen St Osburg's church, next to the Victorian gas cylinder. Before this stands Leigh Mills at the top of Hill Street and beyond can be seen open countryside yet to be built on. Above the city are barrage balloons, seventy of which hung over Coventry protecting it from low-flying aircraft. This defensive measure was backed up by numerous ack-ack guns which shifted sites every few weeks.

A view of Holy Trinity taken from the Market Tower, *c.* 1943. Luckily with the help of firewatchers and Revd Clitheroe, Holy Trinity survived the Blitz despite numerous bombs and incendiaries destroying buildings only yards away. The church bears a message to the people of Coventry and many remember it: 'It all depends on me and I depend on God.'

Broadgate looking south at 11.05 a.m., *c.* 1945. The air-raid shelter (front centre) will soon be gone, as peace waits on the horizon.

The Revd R.T. Howard conducts the VE Day (Victory in Europe) service in the ruins of Coventry Cathedral, 8 May 1945. The people of Coventry had lost many citizens in combat and 1,236 at home. The city endured 41 air-raids between 18 August 1940 and 3 August 1942 and had 373 siren alerts.

A military parade passing the Council House, 7 September 1946. The parade was part of a week's fund raising for the army benevolent fund.

The 4.55 to Bedworth picking up passengers outside the remains of Burtons in Broadgate, *c.* 1946.

Broadgate, 1946. The rubble of the city had been cleared away and some sort of normality had returned. Behind Burtons it was like a cornfield, as seeds from a bombed seed merchant's grew here. Buses could only ply Broadgate, for the tram-lines were so badly damaged during the raid of November 1940 that it was decided to scrap the service early, it having originally been the Council's intention to scrap it by 1942.

The lord mayor, Alderman George Briggs, unveiling the Levelling Stone, 8 June 1946. The stone, carved with a phoenix rising, marked the beginning of the rebuilding of the city centre. Donald Gibson, the architect responsible for the project, heard one night of the Ministry of Planning's permission to get the stone and immediately jumped into his car and drove to the Lake District, found a suitable piece of Cumberland granite and arranged for its delivery.

The spires of Holy Trinity and St Michael's rise above the shell of Owen Owen in Cross Cheaping. It was decided in July 1942 to demolish the burnt-out store (despite the exterior looking in perfect condition) and work got underway in mid-1943.

A view of the demolition work from the other side in Trinity Street, looking up into Broadgate. Just ahead of the man on the left is the flower-bed in front of Holy Trinity.

The Grove by the War Memorial Park, *c.* 1941. Out of shot on the right stood (until the 1960s) Styvechale Toll House from which, with the help of a large white gate, the traffic on this eighteenth-century turnpike road was controlled. The Grove (centre) is a very ancient site which may have begun life as a pre-Christian sacred tree-grove. Note the war memorial on the right.

Looking at the Burges and Corporation Street from the bottom of Bishop Street, *c.* 1948. The building in the centre, built in 1932, now called the Tally Ho was then the Wine Lodge. The Automatic Sports Arcade on the right was previously the premises of Fearis & Co., provisions and confectioners. The building, which dates from the eighteenth century, was demolished in the 1960s.

This view of Cheylesmore Manor gatehouse in the 1940s shows half of the ancient gateway up To Let while the right hand side houses the premises of A. Blockley, blind and curtain maker, carpenter and undertaker. This view can now be seen from under the arch in New Union Street.

This shows the view from the other side of the gateway. The building attached to the gate held remains of the original manor house which was built after the decline of Coventry Castle.

SECTION SEVEN

The Fifties and Sixties 1950–1965

Broadgate in the mid-1960s. Between the Godiva Clock and Broadgate House is Hertford Street, straddled by the Bridge Restaurant. Here diners could enjoy a meal while traffic passed under their feet.

Looking down New Street up St Michael's Avenue, *c.* 1950. Much of New Street survived the bombing with varying degrees of damage. The fourteenth-century building on the right called The House of the Cross was thought to have originated as a medieval chapel. Despite its history, it, like the rest of the remains of medieval New Street, was demolished in the 1950s.

Cheylesmore Manor Gatehouse (now the register office), 1953. Underneath the white plaster-work lay a fifteenth-century timber-framed building, occupied as two individual houses either side of the archway. In the background on the left can be seen the roof of a building (demolished 1956) which stood at the site and contained fragments of the original manor house, a thirteenth-century building which, however, was much larger and consisted of a long hall, half sandstone and half timbered.

The Great Fair at the War Memorial Park, Saturday 18 June 1955. The fair, which followed the Coventry Carnival, originally came after the Godiva Procession, which began in 1678.

A corner of the Great Fair, June 1955. With the war ten years in the past, its memories and exploits were kept alive with such shows as seen here. Lieutenant Commander Ian Fraser VC, with the backing of the Royal Navy, shared the wartime experience through underwater re-enactments with frogmen, all for the price of 3d.

The County Hall in Cuckoo Lane, *c.* 1955. This building, the only eighteenth-century public building to survive, was built between 1783 and 1784 when the adjoining prison was remodelled. The prison governor's house still exists attached to the hall. In the eighteenth century four members of what became known as the Coventry Gang were held here in the gaol and guarded by a regiment of soldiers. The extra security was due to the fact that these men and women belonged to a London-based gang some two hundred strong and it was feared a mass storming of the gaol would take place. The last public execution took place here in 1849 (off photo right) and the murderess Mary Ball was buried 16 ft below the prison courtyard where she may still be to this day.

Looking down Hales Street between the Hippodrome and the fire station during the rush-hour, 1958. Between the station and Holy Trinity School was the entrance to Pool Meadow.

A sunny Saturday afternoon in July in the mid-1960s as the carnival procession passes before Holy Trinity church in Trinity Street. The city carnival was once a great event of civic pride, with hundreds of floats supplied by the city's many manufacturing firms. Note the men standing on top of the scaffolding on St Michael's spire.

Acknowledgements

I would like to thank Heather Head for proofreading and other invaluable work, Paul Harrison and Jeff Langbridge for photographic work, and John Drittler, C.M. Barlow, James Armer, Trevor Pring and H. & J. Buust for photographs. Also special thanks to Dennis Beasley, Neil Cowley, Tereza Cliff and Coventry Local Studies, Central Library, for their continuing assistance.